Getting dressed for SEASONS

STICKER ACTIVITY BOOK

Om KIDZ
An imprint of Om Books International

It's winter! The weather is
very chilly and cold.

Using your stickers help Kiara and Josh stay warm so they can enjoy the day, play around with their pets and the snow!

It's fun to ski and skate on the snow and ice. Paste the stickers and add to the enjoyment of the children!

Liza and Polly love the pitter patter
of rain drops. Help them dress up so
they can enjoy the rainy day.

Pg-2
Pg-3
Pg-4
Pg-5

Pg-5
Pg-6
Pg-7

Pg-9
Pg-10
Pg-11
Pg-12

Pg-14
Pg-13
Pg-15
Pg-16

Kim and Susie are playing in the rain.
Join them in the fun by adding your stickers!

Spring is the time for blooming flowers. Sam has plans to fly kites and Jill has to water her plants. Dress them up so they can go about enjoying this pleasant day!

What are Susan and her friends doing on this summer evening? Paste the stickers and find out.

Help Jim and Tiara get ready for this fine fall day, so they can finish up their work!

What clothes can the scarecrow wear to scare away the birds? Let your stickers dress it up!